SPORTS'
TOP
MVPS™

AARON RODGERS

PHILIP WOLNY

rosen publishing's
rosen
central®

New York

Published in 2019 by The Rosen Publishing Group, Inc.
29 East 21st Street, New York, NY 10010

Library of Congress Cataloging-in-Publication Data

Names: Wolny, Philip, author.
Title: Aaron Rodgers / Philip Wolny.
Description: New York : Rosen Publishing, 2019. | Series: Sports' Top MVPs | Includes bibliographical references and index. | Audience: Grades: 5–8.
Identifiers: LCCN 2017044963| ISBN 9781508182108 (library bound) | ISBN 9781508182115 (paperback)
Subjects: LCSH: Rodgers, Aaron, 1983—Juvenile literature. | Football players—United States—Biography—Juvenile literature. | Quarterbacks (Football)—United States—Biography—Juvenile literature.
Classification: LCC GV939.R6235 W65 2019 | DDC 796.332092 [B] —dc23
LC record available at https://lccn.loc.gov/2017044963

Manufactured in the United States of America

On the cover: Aaron Rodgers drops back to pass against the Houston Texans at Lambeau Field on December 4, 2016.

CONTENTS

It was a sunny day in September 2014 when Annie Bartosz got a big surprise. Bartosz was in her hometown of Hartfield, Wisconsin. A camera crew was there, but she was used to them. In late 2012, she had started Gold in September, or G9, when she was just eleven years old. The group was a pediatric cancer awareness charity dedicated to her brother. He had died of a rare kind of cancer that year.

A smiling, athletic man came over to help Annie with her on-camera makeup. When he sat down with her, she lit up. She recognized the man: it was none other than Super Bowl champion quarterback and Most Valuable Player (MVP) Aaron Rodgers! Together, Annie and Rodgers went door to door in her neighborhood to try to get donations and other support for her organization.

This was just one example of giving back for Rodgers. Of course, the fame that Rodgers brings to his charity work comes from his work on the football field. It is there, on the gridiron, that Rodgers has proven that he is one of the greatest professional players of all time and certainly one of the most successful and accomplished quarterbacks.

Rodgers has been a hot commodity, with great expectations surrounding him. He led his team, the National Football League's (NFL) Green Bay Packers of Green Bay, Wisconsin, to a Super Bowl victory, which also earned him a Super Bowl Most Valuable Player (MVP) award. He has also been the NFL's season MVP twice and has scored standing records in passing and touchdown-to-interception statistics, among many other milestones.

All the while, he has worked his way steadily upward to the highest ranks of football and sports MVPs in general. But the Chico, California, native has also been a frequently

Green Bay Packers quarterback Aaron Rodgers raises the Vince Lombardi Trophy at Cowboys Stadium in Arlington, Texas, while celebrating his team's Super Bowl win on February 6, 2011.

underestimated underdog. He had to step up and prove himself a capable team leader when an older, legendary quarterback suddenly left the team. Fans were unconvinced and suspicious of the newcomer at first. But Rodgers brought to Green Bay the persistence, hard work, and spirit that had brought him success from high school football to college and then on to the NFL.

Like any player with longevity—the ability to maintain career success season after season—Rodgers has faced injury, minor controversy, and bad luck but has managed to come out on top. In addition, he has learned from his experiences and has earned a reputation as a private, thoughtful, and caring athlete on and off the field. Here is the story of Aaron Rodgers, one of football's (and sports') greatest MVPs.

CHAPTER ONE

TALENT SHINES THROUGH

On December 2, 1983, Edward and Darla Rodgers welcomed their second son, Aaron, into the world in Chico, California, a small city about 90 miles (145 kilometers) north of the state's capital, Sacramento. Aaron had a comfortable and love-filled childhood. His father, Edward, originally from Texas, eventually became a chiropractor specializing in sports injuries. His career path was likely influenced by Edward Rodgers's successes on the offensive line of the California State University Wildcats. He even received all-conference honors. This led to some time playing semiprofessional ball, too, which he gave up for a chiropractic career.

Rodgers gets ready to toss the football during a warm-up session before a September 2017 matchup against the Cincinnati Bengals.

THE FOOTBALL HERO AS A TODDLER

Aaron, alongside his older brother, Luke, and younger brother, Jordan, were introduced to football and other sports early. It was not only Edward Rodgers's athletic abilities, however, to which many sportswriters attribute Aaron's success. His mother, Darla, was an accomplished college basketball player and a dancer, too. She told Green Bay's FOX6 in 2013 about all her boys, "I think that my guys did get some of my dancer qualities." Both parents think they gave their sons just enough competitive drive and exposure to sports but not too much.

There are different accounts of when Aaron became interested in sports, and football specifically—some say as early as his third, or even second, birthdays. At an age when most kids can barely sit still for five minutes, Aaron could supposedly sit through an entire NFL game on television. This meant watching his favorite team, the San Francisco 49ers, especially legendary quarterback Joe Montana. He was also an avid football card collector and could even memorize and talk about football statistics.

By Aaron's fifth birthday, family members and friends recollect, Aaron could throw a football through a tire swing. He could also identify various playing formations that the 49ers used. Family friend Larry Ruby told the *New York Times* in 2011, "That's when I began thinking his mind was really amazing and his physical attributes were phenomenal."

A NATURAL ATHLETE

Aaron loved sports and pushed himself to compete, especially against his older brother, who was just about a year and a half his senior. While supportive of their football dreams, their father told them to delay playing until high school, fearing his boys would hurt themselves or simply dedicate too much of their childhoods to it.

Aaron also showed his athletic abilities as a pitcher in Little League baseball, especially the strong arm that made him famous years later. Aaron was relatively small and thin, and until people saw his fastball, he was often initially dismissed. He played for the Raleigh Hills Little League in Beaverton, Oregon. The family moved there temporarily in the mid-1990s so that Ed could continue his training as a chiropractor.

Working very hard, whether it's during a game or just a warm-up, is one of the hallmarks of Rodgers's football career.

Aaron also played basketball. Later, as an adult, he credited his diverse skills on the football field partly to playing different sports. He told the *Philadelphia Inquirer* in 2017, "It definitely helped me because I learned different skills in different sports, and there are competitive things that run through all the sports." For example, when talking about his later skill in throwing completions, he said, "With the different arm angles, that's baseball." He added, "I can see basketball helps with your footwork in the pocket and your movement and your base."

HIGH SCHOOL HERO

By the time Aaron entered eighth grade, the Rodgerses had returned to Chico. Aaron convinced his father to let him play football. In ninth grade,

Pleasant Valley High School students cheer hometown hero and school alumnus Rodgers during a pre–Super Bowl rally at the school's gym on February 4, 2011.

as a freshman at Pleasant Valley High School in his hometown, Aaron was smaller than most successful high school football players. He was completely average, at a height of 5 feet 2 inches (1.57 meters) and weighing 130 pounds (59 kilograms). But he was still smaller than many athletes who go on to successful professional careers.

While he had something to prove due to his size, friends, teammates, and coaches saw signs of something special in Aaron. A friend gave him the nickname Hurley. It was a reference to the skinny but spectacular basketball point guard Bobby Hurley, who played for the Sacramento Kings. It was another sign that while Aaron may not have been 6 feet (1.83 m) tall and 200 pounds (90.7 kg), he was still going places.

It was his junior year when Aaron really got the chance to shine. While other students balanced academics and social lives, Rodgers kept

OFF THE FIELD: A GOOD STUDENT

Aaron excelled off the field as well. One unfortunate and unfair stereotype of many athletes is that they are not as bright as they are athletically talented. In reality, athletes score all over the map when it comes to academics. Aaron was an all-around talent in many of the things he did.

Rodgers claimed to several interviewers that he only once received an F in a school project or subject from grade school through high school—and that was a seed-planting assignment in fourth grade. At Pleasant Valley, his grade point average was an impressive 3.6—about an A- overall—an impressive feat for someone who also trained athletically. He also achieved a 1310 score on the Scholastic Aptitude Test (SAT), out of a possible perfect 1,600 score that existed before the exam was changed in 2005.

partying to a minimum. He knew that he would have to get up for 6 a.m. workouts. That year, he became starting quarterback and continued as a starter his senior year. That is when he set some records at Pleasant Valley that still stand. One was tossing six touchdowns in a single game. Another was for the most passing yards in a single season, 2,303, and the most total yards, too, at 2,466.

Even with an incredible two years as a starting quarterback, Aaron was not guaranteed to go on to play college football. As a good student and great athlete, he hoped to score a football scholarship. The dream for most high school athletes is to get a scholarship or at least land a place on a Division I team. However, in 2002, as graduation approached, Aaron failed to strike up any real interest among scouts. Still wanting to play in college, he decided to attend nearby Butte Community College. The two-year school was only 25 miles (40 km) away from Chico. But the mark he would begin to make there would take Aaron Rodgers as far as he had hoped and dreamed he could go.

CHAPTER TWO

BREAKING OUT AT BUTTE AND BERKELEY

A small, relatively unknown school like Butte College, in Oroville, California, might seem an unlikely place to start a superstar career in the NFL. Butte, which sits on a wildlife refuge, is well known for programs in environmental sustainability, but less so for college athletics. Other players might have been discouraged by going to a school that seemed, to some, like a dead end for someone hoping to go pro.

Still, Aaron Rodgers was in good company there. Powerful NFL guard Larry Allen is one of several football players, along with running back Alex Green of the Green Bay Packers, to have started careers at Butte. For years, the school got a reputation as a last chance for some players, a first chance for others. The school's football stadium did not even have electric lights installed.

A BIG BREAK AT BUTTE

Butte College football coach Craig Rigsbee had actually recruited Rodgers in 2001, in the winter before he graduated from Pleasant Valley. At the time, not many college football scouts wanted to take a chance on a small quarterback. Rodgers was only 5 feet 10 inches

Rodgers, as UC Berkeley quarterback, looks for an opening while passing during the 2003 Big Game, an annual matchup between Berkeley and Stanford University.

(1.77 m) tall and 185 pounds (84 kg). San Diego State had seemed interested, but then its coach was fired, sinking that possibility. Not too many colleges even bothered recruiting in California north of Sacramento. Rodgers even thought about giving up football entirely around that time.

Rigsbee visited the Rodgers home and convinced him otherwise. As Rodgers told the *San Francisco Chronicle* in 2004, "I was kind of down and out about the whole thing, but he gave me my dreams back." The friendly coach was convinced that playing at Butte would help Rodgers to develop. He could then jump to Division I. According to the *Washington Post*, he sold Rodgers on the school's saying "Start here, go anywhere." Most important, Rodgers had a playing style all his own. The young man convinced the older coach to give him the freedom to play his way. Each man took a chance on the other.

A WINNING SEASON

Rodgers would prove Rigsbee's instincts right in the single season he played at Butte. He commuted from Chico, mostly spending time with his hometown friends and his family and was an active member of his family's church. But the mild-mannered Rodgers would lead the Butte Roadrunners to an incredible record of ten wins and only one loss the entire season. Rodgers was declared the team's offensive MVP due to his 26 touchdowns, 2,156 yards, and only four interceptions. Butte would achieve second place in its national rankings. Rodgers would later admit that the winning season gave him a huge boost to his confidence. In addition, he grew three inches that season, growing to 6 feet 1 inch (1.85 m).

Rodgers also took from Butte an appreciation for the game that more professionalized and successful programs might not have given him. Part of it was the strong team dynamic and the camaraderie he felt there. He spoke of his teammates to *Sports Illustrated* in 2010, "You had guys that had been in construction jobs and grocery store jobs and club jobs . . . Some were bounce-back guys or, like me, guys who'd been overlooked. Everybody was hungry. Guys were playing for the love of the game because they didn't want to start in the workplace."

But the budding young quarterback would still have to fight to prove himself. College scouts came up from San Francisco to check out the local talent. He felt overlooked yet again when they recruited a couple of his teammates—but not Rodgers himself. It was a chip on his shoulder that Rodgers would seem to fight against for much of his career.

DIVISION I BOUND

A teammate took a chance and sent footage of himself and Rodgers to football program officials at the University of California (UC) at Berkeley.

A coach there, Jeff Tedford, was impressed with Rodgers's footage. He also saw that the young quarterback made great plays by taking chances other coaches might have advised against. Rigsbee had honored his promise to let Rodgers try things his way. "Not too many people can do some of the things he does," Tedford told the *Washington Post* in 2015.

Tedford hosted a scouting meeting with Rodgers and some other players from Butte shortly after, and then Rodgers got a call that would change his life: Tedford was offering him a scholarship to play football at Berkeley. Luckily, his good grades from high school qualified him to transfer to the new school after just the single season with Butte. He would now play for the California Golden Bears.

Throughout both his college and professional careers, Rodgers has been known for his fine playing under pressure.

AT BERKELEY

At Cal (the nickname for UC Berkeley), Rodgers began the 2003 season as a backup quarterback. In the fifth game that season, he got the starting position. He led the Golden Bears to an overall record of eight wins and six losses. While he played, they won seven games and lost three. Their regular season finished with Rodgers passing for 414 total yards against Stanford. They played the Insight Bowl against Virginia Tech. Despite trailing Tech 21–7, Rodgers rallied the team. He completed 27 of 35 attempted passes, helped the Bears gain 31 points and beat their foes, 52–49, in the final seconds of the game.

PROVING THEM WRONG

Much as he sometimes had to prove sports fans and scouts wrong about his potential, Rodgers encountered a professor at Berkeley who doubted him. The teacher in question even laughed in his face. As *USA Today* reported in 2012 and Rodgers discussed on a weekly radio show he did in Green Bay, he had taken a food appreciation course as part of his degree. He and some others had done a group project together. However, they had received an F on their paper. The teacher said this was because they had improperly cited sources.

Rodgers approached the teacher about doing a rewrite. He had not received a failing grade since elementary school. He explained:

> She went into this tirade about athletes and entitlements . . . She basically picked on the wrong person in the class because I was probably the best student out of the 11 football players in there . . . She's looking at me, condescending, talking down to me. And she says, "What do you want to do with yourself?" I said, "I want to play in the NFL." She laughed at me [and said,] "You'll never make it. You'll get hurt. You'll need your educa-tion, and you're not gonna make it through school here."

The professor was right only about the fact that Rodgers would not complete his degree at Berkeley. But about him becoming a pro football player, she was way off the mark.

During Rodgers's junior year, the Bears' record was even better. They won ten games and lost one. Even during their one loss, Rodgers set a Cal record, completing 26 consecutive passes in one game. Their

Posing with other players at the Jacob K. Javits Convention Center in New York City, Rodgers (*third from left*) takes a photo break during the seventieth annual NFL Draft.

record earned the Bears a slot in the Holiday Bowl against the Texas Tech Red Raiders, though they lost that game. Rodgers was also a finalist for college football's highest honor in 2004, the Heisman Memorial Trophy, awarded to the most outstanding player. Due to all his wins and the buzz around him, Rodgers made the big decision that year not to complete his senior year at Berkeley. Instead, he aimed ever higher at his dream of being a pro. He would enter the 2005 NFL Draft.

CHAPTER THREE

GOING PRO AS A PACKER

E ach year, all the teams of the NFL gather to pick new talent from a pool of available college players. The last place team from the previous year is given first pick, while the winningest teams draw last. Teams make various deals and exchanges within the larger draft, and the draft consists of seven rounds of each team selecting players.

The 2005 NFL Draft at first seemed to be very promising for Aaron Rodgers. Mock online draft predictions made many people think Rodgers would be among the top five picks—that is, he would be among the first five selected. Some even believed he could be the top draft pick that year.

When it was held in April 2005 in New York City, however, Rodgers had to wait a little while to be picked. He was not picked until the twenty-fourth selection of the first round. It was the Green Bay Packers that selected him for their team. He had made it to the NFL.

BIG SHOES TO FILL

That year, Rodgers started as a backup quarterback at Green Bay. He spent much of his time on the bench. The legendary Packers quarterback Brett Favre was still the starter. He had started every game

Ted Thompson, general manager of the Green Bay Packers, poses with Rodgers at an April 2005 press conference.

for the team since September 1992. It was not the first time that Rodgers had to sit back and wait for his chance at greatness. While waiting, he helped quarterback the defensive practices. Some players even thought he practiced too hard.

Rodgers suffered a minor setback his second season when he broke his foot. He spent little time on the field as it was. Things continued more or less the same until the off season in 2008. That March, Brett Favre announced his decision to retire from football. The veteran had thrown a devastating interception in the Packers' losing NFC championship game against the New York Giants that past January. He was nearing the end of his career. Rodgers kicked things into overdrive and used the rest of the off season and preseason to prepare. He hoped to do well in his first season starting for the Packers. But things would soon get complicated.

In an odd turn of events, Favre tried to rejoin the Packers. He even showed up to training camp that year. But they traded him to the New York Jets. Rodgers was finally a starter as of 2008, but the way it happened left a bad taste in the mouths of some fans. Many loyal Packers fans insulted Rodgers online and on the field. He would have to work twice as hard to prove himself to these skeptics. He wanted to contribute as much and prove himself as good a quarterback as Favre had been.

PAYING HIS DUES AND RISING TO THE OCCASION

In the first game he played in 2008, Rodgers led the Packers to a 24–19 victory over the Minnesota Vikings. The Packers won the following week against the Detroit Lions. Overall, however, the first season Rodgers started was not a winning one. The previous year with Favre had seen them win thirteen and lose three, and gain a playoff spot. Rodgers's first season as leader of the team ended with a 6–10 record, a losing season. However, Rodgers's personal statistics were very good. He had 4,038 passing yards and 28 touchdowns.

Some journalists pointed out that Rodgers found it hard to win close contests. Between getting booed by fans—even at hometown Lambeau

TEAMMATES AND COACHES ON RODGERS

Linebacker A. J. Hawk told *Sports Illustrated*: "We've seen him go through a pretty unique situation. We saw how well he handled it, how he never lashed out . . . I think he's the poster child on how to handle a tough situation."

Wide receiver Greg Jennings told *Sports Illustrated*: "Now he's at the point where he trusts himself and the guys around him. He plays with a certain confidence and a certain swagger, which he should. You can't play timid, especially at that position."

Former Butte Community College football coach Craig Rigsbee told the *Dallas News*: "This whole thing, I don't want to say it's cosmic, but it has lined up for him . . . He always had these roadblocks, but he quietly overcame them. That made him better."

Former Cal head coach Jeff Tedford told ABC News 7 reporter Mike Shumann: "He's a phenomenal player, and the leadership he provides, and the coolness, and the way he handles things is phenomenal."

Field—and getting criticized for not being Brett Favre, it was a rough year. Rodgers told *Sports Illustrated* in 2010 that he grew a mustache because the "questions got old, and I realized that if I could cut my facial hair into something crazy, maybe they'd ask me about that and every question wouldn't be about the guy who played before me."

In 2009, things started to improve in a big way for both Rodgers and the Packers. Besides leading the Packers to an 11–5 record and a bid in the playoffs, Rodgers got even better. He seemed more confident. With time, he and his teammates learned each others' rhythms and how to work together well. In addition, with 4,434 passing yards that season, Rodgers officially became the first to throw at least 4,000 yards in each of his first two seasons as starting quarterback.

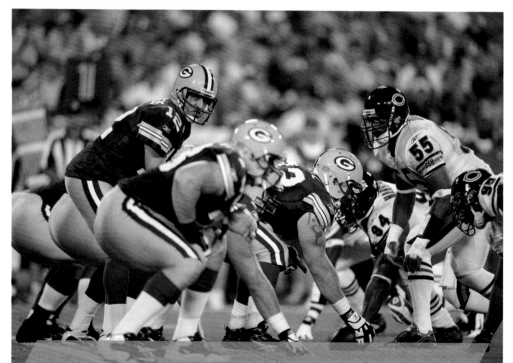

Rodgers gets ready to make a play as the Packers face off against the Chicago Bears during a home game on September 13, 2009.

With that good record, Rodgers helped get the Packers to the play-offs. They played in the wild card round against the Arizona Cardinals (the wild card round being the two best teams in each conference that do not win their divisions facing off against each other). It was one of the highest-scoring postseason games in NFL history. While Rodgers and his opposing quarterback, Kurt Warner, gave it all they had, the game went into overtime, tied at 45–45. But Rodgers was sacked and fumbled the ball. It was scooped up by the Cardinals' Carlos Dansby. Dansby ran 17 yards to score the winning touchdown.

CHAPTER FOUR

SUPER BOWL CHAMP AND MVP

For the 2010 season, Rodgers was ready to build on the previous year's successes. It would be a tough season, though, and not only for the star quarterback. Several players sat out multiple games due to injuries or did not come back for the season. Linebackers Nick Barnett, Brad Jones, Brady Poppinga, and Brandon Chillar all got hurt. So did starting end Cullen Jenkins, with an injured hamstring. Up to twenty-five players were on injured reserve throughout the season. This included Rogers's own brushes with two concussions, which affected a couple of games.

A CHAMPIONSHIP SEASON

All the naysayers who had doubted that Rodgers could take over for the veteran Favre were soon to be proven wrong. With injuries and other struggles, the Packers ended up with a 10–6 record for the regular season. Few teams that just barely squeak by and get into the playoffs end up going all the way to the Super Bowl. Still, most every game that Rodgers and his teammates lost was very close in terms of scores.

The Packers qualified for the NFC wild card game against the Philadelphia Eagles. Their 21–16 victory earned them the spot playing the Atlanta Falcons in the NFC divisional matchup. After a strong beginning from Atlanta, Rodgers's Packers racked up 35 points in just eighteen minutes of playing time. He avoided multiple sack attempts by the Falcons. By the end, Green Bay stood victorious, 48–21. Looking back, Rodgers still thinks of this game against Atlanta as one of his best performances ever.

Next, Rodgers would face the Chicago Bears in the NFC Championship. Rodgers's arm remained one of the Packers' best weapons. He completed about 71 percent of his passes in the postseason. The Bears' defense kept their opponents from scoring too high in their face-off. But they fell, too, 21–14.

Zach Kruse, a sports blogger wrote on The Packers Wire site, "Aaron Rodgers' incredible run during the 2010 NFL playoffs still

A victorious Rodgers gestures to fans while relishing a win in the NFC playoffs over the Atlanta Falcons on January 15, 2011.

holds up as one of the most dominant stretches of individual quarterback play in postseason history." For fans, it seemed a magical run-up to the eagerly awaited return of the Packers to the Super Bowl.

SUPER BOWL XLV

The Super Bowl is always a huge event. For any player, it is the biggest game of a career. For Rodgers, especially, it was his chance to show that he was as good as Brett Favre and to show that he deserved his recent success. A loss after their tough season would have been especially heartbreaking.

TAKING PUNISHMENT

Bad luck with injuries in 2010 seemed infectious for Green Bay's quarterback. In October, Rodgers suffered a concussion during an overtime game against the Washington Redskins. He was hit by three players at the same time. They lost that game, but Rodgers played the following week. That December, while playing against the Detroit Lions, Rodgers was sacked twice in a row. He stayed in for a while, not truly realizing how badly he was hurt. In many ways, he was lucky. Many players shake off trauma because they want to help their team win. Sometimes this can threaten players' health and even their lives. "It's just kind of what's built into you," Rodgers told *USA Today* in 2016. "I went back out there for a couple plays, and I couldn't call the plays, and they ended up getting me out of there." Another quarterback took over, and the Lions beat the Packers 7–3.

Both the Packers and the Steelers struggled early in the game. But then Rodgers threw a touchdown catch to Jordy Nelson. A later Packers interception and another touchdown pass from Rodgers to Greg Jennings in the second quarter left Green Bay with a big lead of 21–3. But the Steelers would rally and get very close to tying the game.

Rodgers remained calm and cool under pressure, though. In the fourth quarter, Rodgers connected with Jennings again. The Steelers rallied, too, but could not quite inch their way back on top. The end of the night saw the Packers prevail, 31–25. Rodgers had achieved one of his greatest dreams: he and his fellow Packers were the champions of Super Bowl XLV. He even received the top honor that Brett Favre himself had not achieved in his 1997 win for the team in Super Bowl XXXI in 1997: Rodgers was declared that Super Bowl's MVP. He also earned the title of NFL MVP for the year, an honor traditionally bestowed by the Associated Press media organization.

Linebacker Clay Mathews embraces Rodgers as the two teammates celebrate their Super Bowl XLV triumph over the Pittsburgh Steelers on February 6, 2011.

AFTER THE SUPER BOWL: A STELLAR CAREER

Expectations have been high for Rodgers since that Super Bowl win. Even though the Packers have not yet repeated that success, Rodgers has played well in the seasons since. The championship Packers started the 2011 season as heavy favorites to reach—and win—the Super Bowl. Incredibly, they would go on to win 15 games and only lose a single one in the regular season. They were the number-one seed going into the playoffs, which means they skipped the first round of playoffs and faced the New York Giants, with their own star quarterback, Eli Manning. It was a shock for many fans when the Giants crushed Rodgers's hopes to repeat the magic of the previous season and return to the Super Bowl. The Packers suffered a 20–37 at-home loss in front of fans at Lambeau Field.

It seemed just bad luck that the Packers could seem so unstoppable and yet be knocked out of the running just one game into the playoffs. Despite this, Rodgers's playing was so good that he received one of the top honors of the game: he was declared NFL MVP for the 2011 season.

In 2012, Rodgers helped his team achieve an 11–5 record and an impressive showing in the NFC wild card game against the Minnesota Vikings (beating them 12–5). This was also the first home-field playoff victory of Rodgers's career. Unfortunately, the San Francisco 49ers would go on to defeat the Packers in the divisional game that year.

STUMBLES AND A COMEBACK

In April 2013, Rodgers's contract was up for renegotiation. Management ended up signing Rodgers to a salary worth $110 million over five years. It was the biggest deal made by any NFL player up to that point. Fans and teammates expected Rodgers to deliver on the confidence that his bosses had in him.

Another dose of bad luck benched Rodgers, however. While playing against the Bears in week nine of the 2013 season—a game they lost 27–20—Rodgers was sacked. He left the game, and it was reported later that he would be out of commission due to a fracture of his collarbone. He missed seven games during a crucial part of the season. It seemed a miracle when the team made it to the wild card game against San Francisco after an 8–7–1 record (their tie was the first tie for the Packers since the 1980s), a game they unfortunately lost.

The 2014 season saw Rodgers come back fighting. His usually strong play and leadership brought the Packers back to championship con- tention. Their 12–4 record earned them a playoff slot. Their divisional showdown with the Dallas Cowboys saw them victorious, 26–21. But hopes of a Super Bowl spot were dashed the following week. A

Rodgers poses with his MVP trophy alongside NFL commissioner Roger Goodell during a news conference the day after the 2011 Super Bowl.

hard-fought struggle against the Seattle Seahawks ended up going into overtime, but Rodgers and his teammates lost, 22–28.

Rodgers's own accomplishments that season were outstanding, too. He had completed 341 of 520 passes and had passed for 4,381 yards. He also had thirty-eight touchdowns (ranking third among quarterbacks) and a mere five interceptions. Rodgers had even finished up the season while recovering from a calf injury. For the second time in his career, the AP awarded him its MVP award for the season.

CHAPTER FIVE

RODGERS LOOKS FORWARD

Rogers faced his share of new problems and setbacks after his second MVP season in 2014. The Packers did, too. He has proved himself one of the greatest quarterbacks in the game. But fans and writers wonder why that has not resulted in championships and Super Bowl victories. The 2015 loss to the Seahawks in the NFC title championship game was one of his poorer playoff showings. His career, however, has shown that good things come to those who not only wait but work hard and overcome criticism and obstacles.

A LONG, STRANGE 2016

The Packers 2016 season saw Rodgers and company as favorites to make it to the Super Bowl again. They started out with a shaky record, though, and lost four games in a row midseason. But Rodgers helped lead his squad to a six-game winning streak to finish out the season, helping them win their division. Two playoff wins—against the Giants and the Dallas Cowboys—had fans buzzing about Rodgers taking his team to the Super Bowl again. But these hopes were dashed in the NFC championship game, when the Atlanta Falcons crushed them 21–44.

Snow falls as Rodgers departs the football field after losing the 2015 NFC championship game to the Seattle Seahawks on their home turf at CenturyLink Field on January 18.

As sportswriter Jimmy Carlton wrote on OnMilwaukee.com, "It was a year in which Rodgers' ability was questioned and his leadership was doubted repeatedly; that is, until the two-time MVP flipped the superpower switch . . . putting forth one of the greatest stretches of quarterback play in football history." Again, Rodgers had risen to the occasion, even if his team had fallen just short of triumph.

GEARING UP

Rodgers continues to inspire high hopes among fans and football commentators alike. In a 2017 preview of the upcoming season, *Sports Illustrated* featured Rodgers on one of its four covers. The magazine favored the

IN AND OUT OF THE SPOTLIGHT

Rodgers has kept much of his private life under wraps. Being one of the NFL's most famous faces has not made that easy. He has also spoken very cautiously with interviewers, especially sports journalists. It is easy to take things out of context, and today's online culture makes rumors and half-truths spread like wildfire. Whether the subjects are his relationship with his family or a long-term relationship he ended with actress Olivia Munn, Rodgers has tried to keep his private affairs out of the spotlight.

He told ESPN that the most hurtful things were pieces that assumed that his girlfriend or other people somehow were hurting his football career or his family relationships. "When somebody thinks of you a certain way that's not real, or says something about you that's not true, I ... you know, that's not me," he told them. "You're not seeing me the right way."

Packers for the NFC championship. After a good start, a collarbone injury sidelined Rodgers in week six. He was out for seven games, and his team had one of its worst showings. It was the first time since 2008 that the team did not make the playoffs at all.

However winning or difficult a season is, Rodgers always approaches the new one with optimism—confident that good things will happen. "I'm a very optimistic person," he told ESPN, "so I feel like we're going to win it every single year. So it hasn't happened most years. But this is the fun part. There's just so many different things that have to come together." He pointed out that the team has nearly tied the record for most consecutive years reaching the playoffs. At the same time, Rodgers hopes for success and feels good about their chances of getting to the Super Bowl again soon.

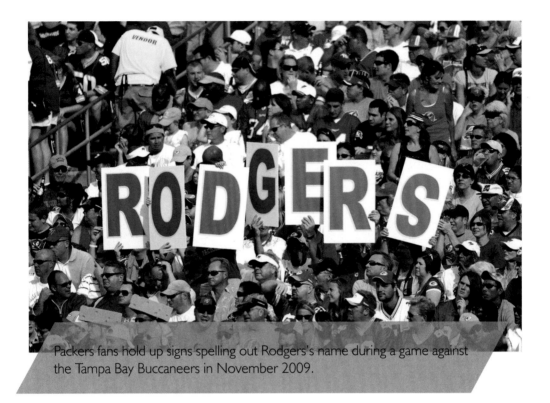

Packers fans hold up signs spelling out Rodgers's name during a game against the Tampa Bay Buccaneers in November 2009.

LIFE AFTER FOOTBALL

Rodgers has thus far had an incredible and much-envied professional record. Many fans and writers consider him the greatest quarterback of his generation. Some have even studied footage of his games and concluded that—without even considering how well the receiver or other players played—Rodgers has been one of the most accurate and skilled quarterbacks season after season. He is famous for his low interception rate and for keeping cool and delivering great throws repeatedly under great stress. So far, only eleven other quarterbacks have thrown more career touchdowns than Rodgers. A *Guardian* article also said, "He's also a very intelligent quarterback, something that is regularly discussed, and possesses rare ability to maximize his pass protection with his footwork, something that is never discussed."

GIVING BACK

One way that Rodgers uses his celebrity for good is through his work with charitable organizations. Since May 2010, Rodgers has been very vocal and involved with the Midwest Athletes Against Childhood Cancer (MACC) Fund. Rodgers told the *Green Bay Press Gazette* in 2015 that a child he met while attending Butte Community College became an early inspiration to him. The boy, Daniel, had leukemia, a life-threatening form of cancer that attacks the immune system. "Learning about the stuff he had to go through: weekly checkups and getting his blood drawn, chemotherapy, how it affects families. That had a big impact on me," he said.

Another child whose story and family inspired Rodgers was Jack Bartosz. Bartosz was only ten when he passed away from a rare form of cancer he had been battling for more than six years. Rodgers became friendly with Jack through MACC. Later, he supported Jack's sister, Annie, and the charity she founded with her parents' help, Gold in September. He even featured her in the first episode of the third season of a public service campaign called itsAaron. He surprised her in her backyard, and they filmed their efforts knocking on doors and talking to people in her area about childhood cancers.

ItsAaron, which Rodgers cofounded with Milwaukee, Wisconsin, lawyer David Gruber, helps share the stories of people in need and to help worthy causes in the Milwaukee area. It has featured not only anticancer efforts but also the stories of children and families who have lost parents or other family members in the military. One episode even featured Rodgers visiting a big Packers fan, an elementary school dean named Tony Gonzalez, to support his contributions to the community.

Besides hopefully more championships and a return to the Super Bowl, what does Aaron Rodgers plan for long term? He hopes to spend his retirement away from the spotlight once he finishes his playing career.

A gleeful Rodgers reacts to the field goal that gives the Packers a win over the Dallas Cowboys during a 2017 NFC division playoff game.

He told *Sports Illustrated*, "After football? I'd like to semi-disappear. I love the game. The game's been incredible to me. But disappearing's good, too. Disappearing to me is not being on TV, not being on the radio. I'd like to coach somewhere at a high school, trying to help the next generation, trying to help the next kid overcome the odds and be the best he can be." It would be a fitting late in life job for the lifelong underdog and naturally talented quarterback and MVP.

FACT SHEET

Name
Aaron Charles Rodgers
Birth Date
December 2, 1983
Birthplace
Chico, California
High School
Pleasant Valley (Chico, CA)
College
Butte Community College;
University of California, Berkeley
Height
6 feet 2 inches (1.9 m)
Weight
225 pounds (102 kg)
Team
Green Bay Packers

Position
Quarterback
Home Field
Lambeau Field, Green Bay,
Wisconsin
Achievements and Awards
Super Bowl champion (Super Bowl
XLV, 2011)
Super Bowl MVP (XLV, 2011)
NFL MVP (2011, 2014)
Notable Charitable Efforts
Midwest Athletes Against
Childhood Cancer (MACC) Fund;
cofounder of itsAaron
**Off-Field Hobbies and
Interests**
Going to the beach; hiking, golfing

TIMELINE

1983 Aaron Rodgers is born on December 2, in Chico, California.

1989 A five-year-old Rodgers is able to throw passes accurately through a hanging tire in the backyard.

1998 Rodgers attends Pleasant Valley High School, becoming the star quarterback.

2002 Rodgers enrolls in Butte Community College, achieving success as a quarterback for the Roadrunners.

2003 Rodgers is recruited by the University of California at Berkeley, playing for the Golden Bears.

2004 Rodgers becomes a finalist for the coveted Heisman Trophy, college football's highest honor for an individual player.

2005 Rodgers is selected by the Green Bay Packers in the NFL Draft.

2008 Rodgers becomes the starting quarterback for the Packers, replacing legend Brett Favre.

2009 Rodgers becomes the first quarterback to pass for more than 4,000 yards in his first two starting seasons.

2010 His stellar play this season earns Rodgers MVP status.

2011 Rodgers leads the Packers to the championship and to victory in the Super Bowl. He receives the Associated Press's MVP award for the year and is also declared Super Bowl MVP.

2012 Rodgers and the Packers make it to the playoffs yet again but fall short of a Super Bowl appearance.

2013 A promising season becomes a grueling one when Rodgers sits out several games due to an injury. Nevertheless, he leads the Packers to a wild card playoff game, but they lose to San Francisco.

2014 Rodgers's season earns him his second overall MVP title. He marks the beginning of the season with his one hundredth regular season start. He ranks first in NFL history in career touchdown passes, yards, and passer rating.

2016 Rodgers leads the Packers to the NFC championship game against the Atlanta Falcons, but they are beaten.

backup A player who fills in for a starter or other player who gets injured or is otherwise unavailable.

chemotherapy A type of serious medical treatment of cancer using chemicals injected into the patient's body.

condescending Showing an attitude toward another person as if that person is beneath you or less intelligent.

conference In the NFL, the grouping of teams into two groups made up of sixteen teams each—the American Football Conference (AFC) and the National Football Conference (NFC).

Division I The group of college-level sports teams that are considered the best.

draft A process used in sports to decide which players go to which teams.

fumble The act of losing hold of the ball in football.

injured reserve The status of players with a major injury, who are unable to practice or play football for at least six weeks or forty-two days.

interception A forward pass that is caught by the opposing team.

leukemia A life-threatening cancer that damages the immune system.

longevity The state of sticking around for a long time, especially in a sports career.

pediatric Having to do with the medical care of children.

playoffs The series of football games that occur after the regular playing season, leading up to the Super Bowl.

preseason The time before the regular season when a team practices and plays games that do not count officially toward their record.

sack A tackle of the quarterback behind the line of scrimmage.

starter The player in any given position that starts the game, usually playing most or all of it.

wild card Having to do with the two best teams in each NFL conference that are not winners of their divisions. In the wild card games, they are given the chance to play and move forward in the playoffs.

FOR MORE INFORMATION

Canadian Football League (CFL)
50 Wellington Street East, 3rd Floor
Toronto, ON M5E 1C8
Canada
(416) 322-9650
Website: https://www.cfl.ca
Twitter, Facebook, and Instagram: @CFL
The CFL organizes and runs the highest level of professional football
in Canada.

Green Bay Packers
Lambeau Field Atrium
1265 Lombardi Avenue
Green Bay, WI 54304
(920) 569-7500
Website: http://www.packers.com
The Green Bay Packers are one of the most successful and the oldest
NFL franchise in operation with the same name and same location.

Midwest Athletes Against Childhood Cancer, Inc. (MACC) Fund
10000 West Innovation Drive, Suite 135
Milwaukee, WI 53226
(414) 955-5830
Website: https://www.maccfund.org
Facebook: @MACCFund
Twitter: @maccfund
Instagram: @themaccfund
YouTube: @MACCFundInc
This athlete-sponsored nonprofit is dedicated to fighting childhood cancer.

National Collegiate Athletic Association (NCAA)
700 West Washington Street
PO Box 6222
Indianapolis, IN 46206-6222
(317) 917-6222
Website: http://www.ncaa.org
Facebook: @ncaastudents
Twitter: @NCAA
Instagram: @NCAAsports
YouTube: @ncaa
The NCAA is the chief organizing body that runs college-level athletics in
    various sports, including football.

National Football League (NFL)
345 Park Avenue
New York, NY 10154
(212) 450-2000
Website: https://www.nfl.com
The NFL is the premier league for professional football in the United States.

Pro Football Hall of Fame
2121 George Halas Drive NW
Canton, OH 44708
(330) 456-8207
Website: http://www.profootballhof.com
Facebook and YouTube: @ProFootballHOF
Twitter and Instagram: @profootballhof
The Pro Football Hall of Fame is a museum dedicated to the history of
    achievement in professional football.

University of California at Berkeley Golden Bears
Memorial Stadium #4426
Berkeley, CA 94720-4426
Website: http://www.calbears.com
Aaron Rodgers spent two formative years as a college player with the
UC Berkeley Golden Bears, a Division I team.

FOR FURTHER READING

Anderson, Jamson. *Aaron Rodgers*. Minneapolis, MN: ABDO Publishing, 2015.

Bowker, Paul. *Playing Pro Football*. Minneapolis, MN: Lerner Publications, 2015.

Christopher, Matt, and Stephanie Peters. *The Greatest Sports Team Rivalries*. New York, NY: Little, Brown Books for Young Readers, 2012.

Easterbrook, Gregg. *The King of Sports: Football's Impact on America*. New York, NY: Thomas Dunne Books, 2013.

Frisch, Aaron. *Aaron Rodgers*. Mankato, MN: Creative Education, 2013.

Hoblin, Paul. *Aaron Rodgers: Super Bowl MVP.* Minneapolis, MN: ABDO Publishing, 2012.

Maurer, Tracy. *Aaron Rodgers*. North Mankato, MN: Capstone Press, 2016.

Nagelhout, Ryan. *Aaron Rodgers*. New York, NY: Gareth Stevens Publishing, 2014.

Rappoport, Ken. *Peyton Manning: Champion Football Star*. Berkeley Heights, NJ: Enslow Publishers, 2013.

Reischel, Rob. *Aaron Rodgers: Titletown MVP*. Chicago, IL: Triumph Books, 2015.

Sandler, Michael. *Aaron Rodgers and the Green Bay Packers: Super Bowl XLV*. New York, NY: Bearport Publishing, 2012.

Scheff, Matt. *Eli Manning: Football Superstar.* North Mankato, MN: Capstone Press, 2014.

Schuh, Mari C. *Aaron Rodgers*. New York, NY: Bearport Publishing, 2013.

BIBLIOGRAPHY

Adams, Jonathan. "Ed and Darla Rodgers: 5 Fast Facts You Need to Know." Heavy.com, January 22, 2017. http://heavy.com /sports/2017/01/aaron-rodgers-parents-family-dad-mom-ed -darla-jordan-luke-rodgers-brothers-father-mother-who-is-why-latest.

Babb, Kent. "For Aaron Rodgers, Road to the NFL Started at an Apparent Dead End." *Washington Post*, December 15, 2015. https:// www.washingtonpost.com/sports/redskins/for-aaron-rodgers-road-to -the-nfl-started-at-an-apparent-dead-end/2015/12/15/8fe12800-a359 -11e5-ad3f-991ce3374e23_story.html?utm_term=.428942ca0738.

Bukowksi, Peter. "Coming Off Historic 2011 Season, Aaron Rodgers' Run Among Greatest Ever." Bleacher Report, August 29, 2012. http:// bleacherreport.com/articles/1315805-coming-off-historic-2011 -season-aaron-rodgers-run-among-greatest-ever.

Crouse, Karen. "Aaron Rodgers Connects with his Hometown, But the Family Huddle Is Broken." *New York Times*, January 15, 2017. https:// www.nytimes.com/2017/01/15/sports/football/aaron-rodgers-green -bay-packers-nfl-playoffs.html.

Crouse, Karen. "Packers' Rodgers Has Deep Roots in Chico." *New York Times*, January 30, 2011. http://www.nytimes.com/2011/01/31 /sports/football/31rodgers.html.

Fahey, Cian. "Why Aaron Rodgers Is an Even Greater Quarterback Than We Think." *Guardian*, September 5, 2017. https://www.theguardian .com/sport/blog/2017/sep/05/aaron-rodgers-nfl-green-bay -quarterback-statistics.

Florio, Mike. "Aaron Rodgers Pushes Back Against Charges of Packers Mediocrity." Pro Football Talk/NBC Sports, August 7, 2017. http:// profootballtalk.nbcsports.com/2017/08/07 /aaron-rodgers-pushes-back-against-perception-of-packers-mediocrity.

Hack, Damon. "Mr. Rodgers' Neighborhood." *Sports Illustrated*, October 11, 2010. https://www.si.com/vault/2010/10/11/105993226 /mr-rodgers-neighborhood.

Kalland, Robby. "How Aaron Rodgers Went from Not Being Recruited to a Star at Cal." CBSSports.com, September 3, 2015. https://www .cbssports.com/college-football/news/how-aaron-rodgers-went -from-not-being-recruited-to-a-star-at-cal.

Kruse, Zach. "Remembering Aaron Rodgers' Magical Run Through 2010 Playoffs." The Packers Wire/*USA Today*, May 17, 2017. http://packerswire.usatoday.com/2017/05/17 /remembering-aaron-rodgers-magical-run-through-2010-playoffs.

Linnane, Rory. "12 Qs with Aaron Rodgers On Why He Gives Back." *Green Bay Press-Gazette*, October 16, 2015. http://www.greenbaypressgazette.com/story/news /local/2015/10/16/12-qs-aaron-rodgers-life-off-field/74055056.

Meyer, Max. "Aaron Rodgers: I'm Starting Back Nine of My Career." NFL.com, July 11, 2017. http://www.nfl.com/news/story/0ap3000000819381/article /aaron-rodgers-im-starting-back-nine-of-my-career.

Pipines, Tom. "FOX6's Tom Pipines Has Exclusive Interview with Aaron Rodgers' Parents." FOX6, November 21, 2013. http://fox6now .com/2013/11/21/fox6s-tom-pipines-has-exclusive -interview-with-aaron-rodgers-parents.

Sielski, Mike. "Aaron Rodgers' Secret? He Was More Than Just a Quarterback." *Philadelphia Inquirer*, January 21, 2017. http://www .philly.com/philly/blogs/pattisonave/Before-win-over-Eagles-Rodgers -explained-his-greatness-.html.

Slothower, Jen. "Aaron Rodgers Says College Professor Laughed at Him When He Said He Wanted to Play in NFL." NESN.com, October 24, 2012. https://nesn.com/2012/10/aaron-rodgers-says-college -professor-laughed-at-him-when-he-said-he-wanted-to-play-in-nfl.

Spofford, Mike. "Aaron Rodgers Catches Fire in Record-Setting Victory Over Bears." Packers.com, October 20, 2016. http://www.packers .com/news-and-events/article-game-recap/article -/Aaron-Rodgers-catches-fire-in-record-setting-victory-over -Bears/14b24ed7-f763-4967-8997-64e16f8b7edb.

Strauss, Chris. "Aaron Rodgers' Professor: 'You'll Never Make It' in NFL." *USA Today*, October 24, 2012. https://www.usatoday.com/story /gameon/2012/10/24/rodgers-professor-never-succeed/1654723.

Townsend, Brad. "Patience, Perseverance Key for Packers Passer Aaron Rodgers." *Dallas News*, February 1, 2011. https://sportsday .dallasnews.com/dallas-cowboys/superbowlscene/2011/02/01 /patience-perseverance-key-for-packers-passer-aaron-rodgers.

Turczynski, Dan. "Aaron Rodgers: His Rise to Superstardom." Lombardiave.com, October 26, 2012. https://lombardiave .com/2012/10/26/rodgerss-rise-to-superstardom.

Wilde, Jason. "For Aaron Rodgers, Desire to Extend Career Comes from Football 'Love Affair.'" ESPN.com, July 27, 2017. http://www.espn .com/blog/milwaukee/post/_/id/1686/for-aaron-rodgers-desire-to -extend-career-comes-from-football-love-affair.

Wilde, Jason. "Mediocrity? No, But Aaron Rodgers and Packers Want More Titles." ESPN.com, July 27, 2017. http://www.espn.com/blog /milwaukee/post/_/id/1695 /mediocrity-no-but-aaron-rodgers-and-packers-want-more-titles.

Wood, Ryan. "Aaron Rodgers Opens Up About Concussions." Packers News/*USA Today*, July 14, 2016. http://www .packersnews.com/story/sports/nfl/packers/2016/07/14 /aaron-rodgers-opens-up-concussions/87076682.

INDEX

ABOUT THE AUTHOR

Philip Wolny is a writer and editor from Queens, New York City. He has written a wide range of biographies about public figures and celebrities, including hip-hop stars (Sean Combs and Ludacris), authors (James Dashner, Isaac Asimov, Stephen Chbosky), and Afghan president Hamid Karzai.

PHOTO CREDITS